Praise for *The Apostles' Creed*

Ben Myers has given readers a precious gift in this short series of meditations on the Apostles' Creed. Like the Church Fathers whose work permeates this book, he treats us to a series of pithy, pertinent reflections that demonstrate theological depth—yet with a surprisingly light touch. Tackling hard matters like gender and God's fatherhood, the virginal conception, the descent into hell, and the persons of the divine Trinity, Myers is alive to both the richness of Christian tradition and the needs of the hour. This is popular theology in the best sense of that term, making accessible the great truths of the Christian faith.

Oliver D. Crisp
Fuller Theological Seminary,
author of *Saving Calvinism*

Like the Creed, this gem of a book answers the question, "What do Christians believe?" But because it is sensitive to the unique doubts and fears and cynicism of the 21st century, it winsomely answers the question behind that question, "How could Christians possibly believe that?" Myers shows as much as he tells, introducing us to the audacious wisdom of ancient voices whose insights prove timely and perennial. This is the catechesis we need for a secular age, overcoming the forgetting we parade as enlightenment.

James K. A. Smith
Calvin College,
author of *You Are What You Love* and *Awaiting the King*

Ben Myers has written a simple and yet incredibly elegant and sublime account of the Christian faith according to the Apostles' Creed. Myers works through the creed, word by word, phrase by phrase, and explains its meaning afresh in a way that is both memorable and meditative. Drawing on Scripture and the wisdom of church history, Myers teaches us what it means to confess "I believe."

Michael F. Bird
Ridley College, Melbourne, Australia,
author of *What Christians Ought to Believe*

I am very thankful to Ben Myers for his concise, readable commentary on the Apostles' Creed! He joins the refreshing movement that is retrieving the church's long and well-established theological consensus and urging the contemporary church to embrace this wisdom from the past. I am particularly struck by Ben's words: "The truest and most important things we can ever say are not individual words but communal words." His book helps today's church confess the Apostles' Creed as essential truth about the triune God and the salvation he offers.

Gregg R. Allison
The Southern Baptist Theological Seminary,
author of *Historical Theology: An Introduction to Christian Doctrine*

THE
APOSTLES' CREED

THE APOSTLES' CREED

A Guide to the Ancient Catechism

BEN MYERS

LEXHAM PRESS

The Apostles' Creed: A Guide to the Ancient Catechism
Christian Essentials

Lexham Press, 1313 Commercial St., Bellingham, WA 98225
LexhamPress.com

The Harrowing of Hell icon on page 81 is located at St. Andrew Holborn Church in London, England. Used by permission.

Print ISBN 9781683590880
Digital ISBN 9781683590897

Lexham Editorial: Todd Hains, Jeff Reimer, Sarah Awa
Cover Design: Eleazar Ruiz
Typesetting: Brittany Schrock, Abigail Stocker

CONTENTS

CHRISTIAN ESSENTIALS

SERIES PREFACE

The Christian Essentials series passes down tradition that matters.

The church has often spoken paradoxically about growth in Christian faith: to grow means to stay at the beginning. The great Reformer Martin Luther exemplified this. "Although I'm indeed an old doctor," he said, "I never move on from the childish doctrine of the Ten Commandments and the Apostles' Creed and the Lord's Prayer. I still daily learn and pray them with my little Hans and my little Lena." He had just as much to learn about the Lord as his children.

The ancient church was founded on basic biblical teachings and practices like the Ten Commandments, baptism, the Apostles' Creed, the Lord's Supper, the Lord's Prayer, and corporate worship. These basics of the Christian life have sustained and nurtured every generation of the faithful—from the apostles to today. They apply equally to old and young, men and women, pastors and church members. "In Christ Jesus you are all sons of God through faith" (Gal 3:26).

We need the wisdom of the communion of saints. They broaden our perspective beyond our current culture and time. "Every age has its own outlook," C. S. Lewis wrote. "It is specially good at seeing certain truths and specially liable to make certain mistakes." By focusing on what's current, we rob ourselves of the insights and questions of those who have gone before us. On the other hand, by reading our forebears in faith, we engage ideas that otherwise might never occur to us.

The books in the Christian Essentials series open up the meaning of the foundations of our faith. These basics are unfolded afresh for today in conversation with the great tradition—grounded in and strengthened by Scripture—for the continuing growth of all the children of God.

> Hear, O Israel: The LORD our God, the LORD is one. You shall love the LORD your God with all your heart and with all your soul and with all your might. And these words that I command you today shall be on your heart. You shall teach them diligently to your children, and shall talk of them when you sit in your house, and when you walk by the way, and when you lie down, and when you rise. You shall bind them as a sign on your hand, and they shall be as frontlets between your eyes. You shall write them on the doorposts of your house and on your gates. (Deuteronomy 6:4–9)

I BELIEVE IN GOD THE FATHER ALMIGHTY,

maker of heaven and earth,

AND IN JESUS CHRIST, GOD'S ONLY SON, OUR LORD:

who was conceived by the Holy Spirit,

born of the Virgin Mary,

suffered under Pontius Pilate,

was crucified, died, and was buried.

He descended into hell.

On the third day he rose again

from the dead.

He ascended into heaven and is seated

at the right hand of the Father,
and he will come again to judge the
living and the dead.

I BELIEVE IN THE HOLY SPIRIT,

the holy catholic church,

the communion of saints,

the forgiveness of sins,

the resurrection of the body,

and the life everlasting.

AMEN.

PREFACE

he Christian faith is mysterious not because it is so complicated but because it is so simple. A person does not start with baptism and then advance to higher mysteries. In baptism each believer already possesses the faith in its fullness. The whole of life is encompassed in the mystery of baptism: dying with Christ and rising with him through the Spirit to the glory of God. That is how the Christian life begins, and to seek to move beyond that beginning is really to regress. In discipleship, the one who makes the most progress is the one who remains at the beginning. And that is where theological thinking comes in handy. Theology does not have all the right answers, but it can help us to contemplate the reality of baptism and to penetrate more deeply into its meaning for life.

That is why I wrote this book. Not because anyone needs to be told what to believe but because Christ's followers have everything they need already. "All things are yours," says Paul:

"all belong to you, and you belong to Christ, and Christ belongs to God" (1 Cor 3:21–23). We are not beggars hoping for scraps. We are like people who have inherited a vast estate: we have to study the documents and visit different locations because it's more than we can take in at a single glance. In the same way, it takes considerable time and effort to begin to comprehend all that we have received in Christ. Theological thinking does not add a single thing to what we have received. The inheritance remains the same whether we grasp its magnitude or not. But the better we grasp it, the happier we are.

So this small book is an invitation to happiness. I have written it with a glad heart, and I hope it will be helpful for others who want to comprehend the mystery of faith in all its "breadth and length and height and depth, and to know the love of Christ that surpasses knowledge" (Eph 3:18–19).

The book began life as a series of sermons on the creed at Leichhardt Uniting Church in Sydney. I am grateful to the Rev. Dr. John Hirt and to the Leichhardt congregation for their friendship and hospitality on that occasion. To them this book is affectionately dedicated. The sermons were long, and the book is short. In both cases I take comfort from the words of Irenaeus: "Since the faith is one and the same, the one who says much about it does not add to it, nor does the one who says little diminish it."[1]

INTRODUCTION
The Ancient Catechism

On the eve of Easter Sunday, a group of believers has stayed up all night in a vigil of prayer, scriptural reading, and instruction. The most important moment of their lives is fast approaching. For years they have been preparing for this day.

When the rooster crows at dawn, they are led out to a pool of flowing water. They remove their clothes. The women let down their hair and remove their jewelry. They renounce Satan and are anointed from head to foot with oil. They are led naked into the water. Then they are asked a question: "Do you believe in God the Father Almighty?" They reply, "I believe!" And they are plunged down in the water and raised up again.

They are asked a second question: "Do you believe in Christ Jesus, the Son of God, who was born of the Holy Spirit and Mary the virgin and was crucified under Pontius Pilate and

1

was dead and buried and rose on the third day alive from the dead and ascended in the heavens and sits at the right hand of the Father and will come to judge the living and the dead?" Again they confess, "I believe!" And again they are immersed in the water.

Then a third question: "Do you believe in the Holy Spirit and the holy church and the resurrection of the flesh?" A third time they cry, "I believe!" And a third time they are immersed. When they emerge from the water they are again anointed with oil. They are clothed, blessed, and led into the assembly of believers, where they will share for the first time in the eucharistic meal. Finally they are sent out into the world to do good works and to grow in faith.

That is how baptism is described in an early third-century document known as the *Apostolic Tradition*.[2] It points to the ancient roots of the Apostles' Creed. The creed comes from baptism. It is a pledge of allegiance to the God of the gospel—a God who is revealed as Father, Son, and Holy Spirit; a God who is present to us in the real world of human flesh, creating, redeeming, and sanctifying us for good works.

It is often said that creeds are political documents, the cunning invention of bishops and councils who are trying to enforce their own understanding of orthodoxy. In the case of the Apostles' Creed, nothing could be further from the truth. It was not created by a council. It was not part of any deliberate theological strategy. It was a grassroots confession of faith. It was an indigenous form of the ancient church's response to the risen Christ, who commanded his apostles to "make disciples of all nations, baptizing them in the name of the Father and of the Son and of the Holy Spirit" (Matt 28:19–20). The Nicene Creed is a different matter, since it was formulated by two church councils in the fourth century. But even that creed is essentially an enlargement and clarification of the ancient baptismal confession.

Later generations of believers sometimes said that each of the twelve apostles had written one line of the creed—hence the name "Apostles' Creed." It is a charming legend that conveys a deep truth: that the baptismal confession is rooted in the faith of the apostles, and ultimately in the word of the risen Christ himself.

By the second century, the basic form of the creed can be found in widely dispersed Christian communities. Irenaeus, a pastor in second-century Gaul, speaks of a threefold "rule" or "canon" that defines the faith of all Christians throughout the world:

> The church, indeed, though disseminated throughout the world, even to the ends of the earth, received from the apostles and their disciples the faith in one God the Father Almighty, the creator of heaven and earth and the seas and all things that are in them; and in the one Jesus Christ, the Son of God, who was enfleshed for our salvation; and in the Holy Spirit, who through the prophets preached the economies. ... The church ...

carefully guards this preaching and this faith which she has received, as if she dwelt in one house. She likewise believes these things as if she had but one soul and one and the same heart. She preaches, teaches, and hands them down harmoniously, as if she possessed but one mouth. For though the languages throughout the world are different, nevertheless the meaning of the tradition is one and the same.[3]

This rule of faith had two functions. First, it was educational. It formed the basis of catechesis for new believers. In the period of preparation for baptism, new adherents to the Christian faith would memorize the creedal formula and would receive instruction in its meaning. The threefold confession of faith was to be written on the heart so that it could never be lost or forgotten. That way, all believers would have a basic guide to the interpretation of Scripture, and even illiterate believers would be able to retain the substance of the biblical story. They would see Scripture as a unified witness to one God—Father, Son, and Holy Spirit. And they would see the created world as the domain of God's activity: God creates our world, becomes incarnate in it, and will ultimately redeem it fully in the resurrection of the dead. That is how the Christian mind was formed by the ancient catechism.

Second, the rule of faith was sacramental. It was not only used as a catechism in preparation for baptism but was also part of the baptismal rite itself. A person becomes a disciple of Jesus and a member of his community by making the three-fold pledge of allegiance. Baptism is a threefold immersion into the life of God. "The baptism of our regeneration takes place through these three articles, granting us regeneration unto God the Father through his Son by the Holy Spirit."[4] The creedal words are words of power. They are words that perform: like naming a yacht, or making a bet, or speaking a marriage vow. In baptism, something is brought into being as the words are spoken. It is the words, just as much as the water, that make a baptism. By these words a person becomes a disciple of Jesus and a member of his community.

So the creed is both informative and performative,[5] both educational and sacramental. It is a summary of Christian teaching as well as a solemn pledge of allegiance. These two functions of the creed can be distinguished but not separated. Catechesis is necessary so that we can make the baptismal declaration with understanding and with genuine commitment. And in turn the baptismal confession orders our thinking about God and the world.

Even today the creed provides a framework—strong yet surprisingly flexible—for Christian thinking and Christian commitment.

I BELIEVE IN GOD
THE FATHER ALMIGHTY,

maker of heaven and earth.

"I"

he first word is perhaps the strangest part of the whole Apostles' Creed: "I." Who is this I? Whose voice is speaking in the creed?

I have been to wedding ceremonies where the couple write their own vows. It is a recent custom that reflects wider cultural changes. In the past, one of the things that made a wedding special was the fact that you got to say exactly the same words that everybody else said. When a couple said their vows, they weren't just expressing their own feelings. They didn't use their own words; they used the same words that their parents and their ancestors had spoken, and they made those words their own.

But today we are skeptical about the past. We are skeptical about anything that is merely handed down to us. We assume that the truest thing we could ever say would be something we had made up ourselves.

In the same way, Christians today are often suspicious of creeds. Many churches are more comfortable with mission statements than with creeds. The thing about a mission statement is you always get to make it up for yourself. It's like writing your own wedding vows.

But here's the paradox. It is the individualized confession, like the personalized wedding vow, that ends up sounding like an echo of the wider society. What could be more conformist than expressing your feelings of love through your own specially crafted wedding vow? The wedding is a grand occasion, so you want to make it special: but the more you try to personalize it, the more it degenerates into triviality and cliché. The ceremonial quality evaporates. Or again, what could be more conformist than a mission statement? Every company has one. And although each one is unique, they all sound eerily similar, as if all the companies in the world were out to achieve the same blandly generic aims. I think there is a similar dynamic at work in many churches today. The harder they try to be special and unique, the more they seem exactly like everybody else.

By contrast, to confess the creed is to take up a countercultural stance. When we say the creed we are not just expressing our own views or our own priorities. We are joining our voices to a great communal voice that calls out across the centuries from every tribe and tongue. We locate ourselves as part of that community that transcends time and place. That gives us a critical distance from our own time and place. If our voices are still echoes, they are now echoing something from beyond our own cultural moment.

"I believe." Who is the "I" that speaks when we make that confession? It is the body of Christ. It is a community stretched out across history, "terrible as an army with banners" (Song 6:10). The whole company of Christ's followers goes down into the waters of baptism, crying out the threefold "I believe!" In baptism nobody is invited to come up with their own personal statement of belief. All are invited to be immersed into a reality beyond themselves and to join their individual voices to a communal voice that transcends them all.

The truest and most important things we can ever say are not individual words but communal words. Most of the words of my life are trivial and fleeting. They fall from my lips and drift away like dead leaves. But in the creed I am invited to say true words. In confessing the faith of the church, I allow my own individual "I" to become part of the "I" of the body of Christ.

It is then that I am saying something of deep and lasting importance. It is then that my words have roots.

"BELIEVE"

hen politicians make promises, we don't really
expect them to keep their word. We understand
that promises are motivated by self-interest, that
words are tactics to achieve other aims. And we're not just
cynical about other people's promises. We lack confidence in
our own words too. We make solemn promises of lifelong commitment—after signing the prenuptial agreement. Our ability to
trust has been eroded by the sad experience of broken promises, if not by a deeper cynicism about the capacity of words
to bear truth.

Nevertheless, when we say the Apostles' Creed we are
reminded that life itself is founded on trust. Christians in
the ancient church went naked to the waters of baptism. The
second birth is like the first. We are totally dependent. We
bring nothing with us except life. The birth cry of baptism is

the threefold "I believe" of the creed, a cry of total trust in the Triune God.

In North Africa toward the end of the fourth century, Augustine pointed out that life would be impossible without trust. Most of the things we know about the world are really things we believe on the basis of someone else's word. We can't verify for ourselves if events in world history have really happened. But we accept testimonies that have come down to us from the past. We can't visit every location on a map to verify that they all really exist. But we accept the word of others who have been to those places. Closer to home, the family is knit together by trust. I wasn't there to witness the moment of my own conception. If I want to know who my father is, I will have to take my mother's word for it. And I gladly accept her word: I would prefer to trust her than to seek independent verification. It would diminish me as a person if I went around trying to verify everything. Only by adopting an attitude of trust am I able to live and flourish as a human being. Without trust, Augustine says, "we would be unable to do anything in this life."[6]

Obviously not every family is an exemplar of loving trust, and not every parent proves to be trustworthy. But Augustine's point is that we don't have the resources to verify everything for ourselves. Social life is woven together by threads of trust. If I really wanted to live without trust I would need to remove myself from society and live in total isolation. But even then, I would need to rely on tools and technologies that I did not invent and that I do not fully understand. I would need to trust the work of others.

The tragic quality of life comes partly from the fact that human beings are not always trustworthy, yet still we cannot live without trust.

The gospel holds out to us the promise of a totally trustworthy God. Can we verify that promise? Augustine's answer, surprisingly, is yes. Over time we learn that God's promise is worthy of our trust. God's trustworthiness is verified by experience. But we don't start with verification. We start with trust: this leads to experience: and experience leads to knowledge of God's trustworthiness. Augustine says, "If you can't understand, believe, and then you'll understand."[7]

That doesn't mean that Christian belief is an irrational leap into the dark. It is more like tasting a dish that you have never tried. You have seen other people enjoying it; you have read the reviews; the chef swears you'll like it. There are good grounds for trusting, but you will never know for sure until you try it. "Taste and see that the LORD is good," sings the psalmist (Ps 34:8). The first act is an act of trust that gives rise to ever-increasing certainty, which in turn nourishes a deeper and a more knowledgeable trust.

The creed is full of mysterious things. It speaks of things that I can't immediately observe or verify for myself. I believe in God the Creator. I believe in Jesus Christ, God-become-flesh in the midst of creation. I believe in the Holy Spirit, God invisibly transfiguring creation from within. How could I prove the truth of these statements? How could I know for sure? When I take the first step, I start to see the whole world through the eyes of God's promise. I start to live in an environment of trust. And then I learn from experience that God is good—"as good as his word," as the saying goes.

"IN GOD THE FATHER"

What do we believe about God? Right away the creed uses the language of Scripture: God is "Father." It is an echo of revelation when Christians use this word. It is not an idea based on speculation or philosophical reasoning. Jesus reveals God as his "Father." He relates to God as his own Father and invites his followers to share in the same relationship. He calls God "my Father and your Father" (John 20:17), and "your heavenly Father" (Matt 6:14). He teaches his disciples to pray, "Our Father" (Matt 6:9)—that is, to stand alongside Jesus and to address God in the same way Jesus does.

Jesus' relationship to God is unique but also inclusive. His followers stand on the inside of Jesus' unique relationship to God. Jesus calls God "Abba, Father" (Mark 14:36), and his followers are empowered by the Holy Spirit to pray in the same way (Rom 8:15–16). That is what it means to be baptized into the Triune God. By the Spirit we are immersed into the life of Jesus so that we come to share in his position before God.

We speak to God, and God listens to us, as if we were Jesus. Jesus is God's child by nature, and we become God's children by grace. Jesus is born of God; we are adopted. So when we confess that God is "Father," it is not a theological idea but a confession of the defining relationship of our lives. We call God "Father" because that is what Jesus calls God, and because Jesus has invited us to relate to God in the same way. In other words, we call God "Father" because of revelation.

Today many Christians are uneasy about this word. Doesn't it give a privileged place to masculine language? Doesn't it imply that there is gender in God? Doesn't it reinforce the picture of an old bearded man in the sky? These might sound like contemporary concerns. But early Christian teachers were already very sensitive to these problems. They took pains to explain that the Bible uses the word "Father" without any con- notations of gender. In fact, this was one of the things that distinguished Christian belief from ancient pagan ideas about the gods. There was a colorful cast of Greek and Roman gods. Some were male; some were female. They could be passionate, hot-headed, lustful, unpredictable. They could change their minds.

Early Christian teachers were careful to differentiate the God of the gospel from the gods of Greek and Roman culture. The pagan gods are many, but the God of Israel is One. The pagan gods can fly into a rage, but the true God is unchangeable and therefore totally reliable. The pagan gods can be inflamed with lust, but the true God seeks the good of humanity without any self-interest. The pagan gods can arbitrarily turn against human beings, but the true God consistently seeks our good. There was a special word for this in early Christian teaching: God's *philanthropia* (literally "love of humanity"). And while the pagan gods can be male or female, the true God totally transcends gender and the body.

When the fourth-century theologian Athanasius wanted to distinguish Christian belief from the pagan gods, he pointed out that the true God is "by nature incorporeal and invisible and untouchable."[8] In a sermon preached in Constantinople toward the end of the fourth century, Gregory of Nazianzus explained that the words "Father" and "Son" should be used without having any "bodily ideas" in our minds. Otherwise we would be back in paganism, imagining a God who physically procreated in order to bring forth a son. We use the words "Father" and "Son," Gregory says, "in a more elevated sense." We "accept the realities without being put off by the names." Ordinary family connotations cannot be applied to God, much less connotations of gender. "Do you take it," Gregory asks his congregation, "that our God is a male because of the masculine nouns 'God' and 'Father'? Is the 'Godhead' a female because in Greek the word is feminine?" Such crude biological thinking would be pagan, not Christian.[9]

What then does the word "Father" mean? For Christians, the word describes a relationship and nothing more. Here is

Gregory again: "'Father' designates neither the substance nor the activity, but the relationship, the manner of being, which holds good between the Father and the Son."[10] The Father is the source, the origin, the wellspring of divine life. And the Son derives from that source. So there is a relationship of origin between Father and Son. According to early Christian teaching, that is all we are meant to think of when we say the word "Father." We purify our language of all thoughts of gender—otherwise we would be projecting our own assumptions onto God instead of listening to God's self-revelation. "Every bodily thought must be shunned in these matters,"[11] says Athanasius—not because Christians have an aversion to the body but because we have an aversion to the pagan gods!

If the word "Father" refers to a relation of origin within God, then we can draw one important conclusion: God is not only Father but also Son. These words, "Father" and "Son," are relational terms. Neither would make sense without the other. Writing in the second century, Tertullian was the first to develop this simple but important insight: "Father makes son, and son makes father. ... A father must have a son to be a father, and a son must have a father to be a son."[12] When we confess that God is eternally Father, we always have in mind as well the eternal reality of the Son.

"ALMIGHTY"

"P ower" is no longer a nice word. It has a decidedly sinister ring to it. When we speak of power we tend to think of dangerous relationships or of wider systems of domination and control.

But that is not how "might" or "power" is understood in Christian teaching. The early Christians often compared God to a breastfeeding mother: it is a favorite image in numerous sermons and writings from the ancient church. We relate to God not like loyal subjects submitting to a powerful ruler, but like infants drawing nourishment from a mother. God's power is not only above us but also alongside us, beneath us, and within us. It is not the power of subjection and control but a power that frees and enables. Augustine described the divine power as "maternal love, expressing itself as weakness."[13]

This is not like the power of the pagan gods who intervene in the world from time to time. God's might is everywhere present in creation. It is the underlying mystery of everything that exists. It is not just a solution to problems in this world. It is the reason there is a world at all.

We could not really trust in God if God's power were limited, sporadic, or unpredictable. A God who exercised that kind of power would be a pagan god: not the world's sustainer but its invader, or perhaps a distant ruler whose wishes have to be imposed by force.

That is the problem with trying to place any limitations on God's power. If God's power were just one power among others—if God were "mighty" but not "almighty"—then divine power would end up being another form of manipulation or control. Only a God who is totally free and totally sovereign can relate to the world with total love, patience, and generosity. There is power elsewhere in creation: each living thing has its own unique power and energy. But God does not have to compete with these other powers. God's power is their source, the reason why they exist at all. God's power is what sustains and nourishes the power of creatures.

True power is not the ability to control. Controlling behavior is a sign of weakness and insecurity. True power is the ability to love and enable without reserve. God's power, like the power of a good parent or teacher, is the capacity to nourish other agents and to help their freedom to grow. Without the "sovereignty" of a good parent, children have a diminished sense of their own worth and their own agency. In the same way,

God's sovereignty is what secures human freedom, not what threatens it.

In the creed we confess the three great movements of God's power: God lovingly brought the world into being; God lovingly entered the womb and became part of the world in Jesus Christ; and God the Holy Spirit is lovingly transfiguring the world in the lives of the saints.

At every point, God's power is hidden. It is a "gentle omnipotence,"[14] as the British theologian Sarah Coakley has said. God is invisibly almighty in the act of creation, invisibly almighty in the womb of the Virgin, invisibly almighty in the darkness of the tomb, invisibly almighty in the company of believers and in the communal life they share.

The world lives because of this gentle but all-embracing power, and we are free because of it.

"MAKER OF HEAVEN AND EARTH"

I n the second century, Christian teachers struggled to define their beliefs and commitments in opposition to popular rival teachings. The prevailing cultural mood was one of deep spiritual pessimism. Members of the educated class took it for granted that the physical world was inherently evil and irredeemable. They yearned to escape from the world of the flesh and to experience spiritual enlightenment.

Marcion, a charismatic teacher of the second century, had said that the material universe was created by a wicked and incompetent god. Marcion was especially disgusted by the human body, "flesh stuffed with dung" as he called it. Like some of the gnostic teachers of the same period, he was horrified by sex. He viewed procreation as a monstrous evil. Marcion's followers had to adapt their lives to an austere renunciation of sex, marriage, and childrearing. Natural bonds were dissolved; only spiritual bonds were of any value.[15]

Marcion's doctrine was not the only challenge to the emerging Christian movement. The second century witnessed the proliferation of spiritual sects whose adherents were known as gnostics (literally "knowers"). Gnostic teachers claimed to have secret knowledge about the cosmos and the soul. They taught that the physical world was created by an inferior deity and that salvation consisted in escaping from the material world by means of esoteric wisdom. Such teachings were very diverse, but what they had in common was a dualism that divided the (bad) creator from the (good) redeemer and the (bad) world of flesh from the (good) human spirit.

The Christian baptismal confession developed, in part, in response to such world-denying doctrines and the wider culture of despair that had engendered them. Right from the start, Christians were marked by their positive stance toward creation. The Gospel of John begins by retelling Israel's creation story: "In the beginning ..." (John 1:1; Gen 1:1). The followers of Jesus believed that in him they had encountered the enabling source of creation. They had come to know the one through whom "all things were made" (John 1:3). Looking into the face of Jesus, they had seen the blueprint of reality and had come to understand God's good plan for the whole creation.

It was spiritually countercultural to be baptized into this world-affirming faith. The ancient Christians refused to see anything in the world as inherently evil. They confessed that everything in this world has been made by the good and wise God whom they had come to know in Jesus.

Part of the appeal of Gnosticism lay in its response to the problem of evil. Why is there so much evil and suffering in this world? It is, the gnostic teachers reasoned, because the world is the product of an evil god; the very stuff of creation is deficient. That is an elegant solution to the problem of evil. But it raises even worse problems. If previously I had been tormented by experiences of suffering and injustice, after accepting the gnostic doctrine I come to see my very existence as an intolerable injustice. Previously I had been at home in the world and had protested against the disagreeable parts of life. But now I find that the world is no longer my home at all. I am radically alienated from life—the life of all creatures, the life of human society, and my own life. My spiritual existence is a lonely spark of goodness in an overwhelmingly hostile world from which I want to flee and whose destruction I yearn for.

That is how it felt to be a gnostic in the ancient world. I start out wanting a solution to the problem of evil and end up experiencing the whole creation, including my own body, as a vast satanic prison. The gnostic is like a person who sees a red wine stain on the carpet and cannot think of any solution except to cover the rest of the floor in wine. The stain is no longer visible: but at what cost? Gnosticism solves the problem of evil only by transforming everything into evil.

In response to such world-denying visions, early Christian teachers argued that everything in creation is good. Evil, properly speaking, does not exist at all. There are no evil entities, only good ones created by a good God. When a creature fails to be properly itself, when it turns away from its own nature and purpose, then it becomes a deficient version of itself. It is evil to the extent that it now lacks something essential to its own nature. A guitar makes an evil sound when it goes out of tune; its "evil" is not a positive quality but only a deficiency. Or to use the favorite illustration in the ancient church, evil is the absence of good qualities just as darkness is the absence of light. The upshot of all this is that evil cannot be attributed to the Creator. The fourth-century Cappadocian teacher Gregory of Nyssa put it like this: "If a man in broad daylight freely chooses to shut his eyes, it is not the sun's fault when he fails to see."[16]

This is not to say that evil is insignificant. Its consequences are real and devastating. But when we experience those consequences we are experiencing the effects of a deprivation of goodness. Imagine if I were to murder someone by striking them with my reading lamp. The lamp is good when it is used well, and the strength of my arm is a gift of God, but these good things become evil when they are used for the wrong purpose. The consequences of that murder would be very real. There are moral problems here about the way creatures use their freedom, but these are not metaphysical problems about whether creation is good or evil.

Though many evil things happen in this world, Christians confess that we are still living in God's good creation. It is a sick world that needs healing, not an evil world that needs destruction. That is the difference between Christianity and Gnosticism.

It is often said that creeds are narrow and intolerant. But in the ancient world the truth was exactly the opposite. It was the Christian creed that took a stand on behalf of creation. It was the creed that said "no" to those doctrines that condemned creation, disparaged the body, and sought escape from the world of the flesh. Gnosticism was the most comprehensive intolerance imaginable. It was intolerance of the universe and of life and of whatever it means to be human. In saying "no" to Gnosticism, the church says "yes" to the whole material universe.

AND IN JESUS CHRIST, GOD'S ONLY SON, OUR LORD:

who was conceived by the Holy Spirit,
born of the Virgin Mary,
suffered under Pontius Pilate,
was crucified, died, and was buried.
He descended into hell.
On the third day he rose again
   from the dead.
He ascended into heaven and is seated at the
   right hand of the Father,
and he will come again to judge the living
   and the dead.

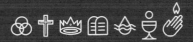

"AND IN JESUS CHRIST, GOD'S ONLY SON, OUR LORD"

We tend to think of creeds as cold didactic summaries of doctrine. But the real centerpiece of the Apostles' Creed is not a doctrine but a name.

Even before the ancient baptismal confession had taken shape, perhaps the earliest Christian confession consisted of just two words: *Kyrios Iēsous*, "Jesus is Lord" (Rom 10:9; 1 Cor 12:3). That early statement remains the spiritual heartbeat of the baptismal creed. Everything else in the creed radiates like the spokes of a wheel from that hub: personal attachment to Jesus; total allegiance to him.

At the center of the Christian faith is not an idea or a theory or even a vision of life but the name of a person, Jesus Christ. Our faith centers on personal attachment to him. A much later Christian confession, the Heidelberg Catechism (1563), gives eloquent voice to the personal center of faith when it begins with the question and answer: "What is your only comfort in life and in death? That I am not my own, but belong—body and soul, in life and in death—to my faithful Savior, Jesus Christ."

Attachment to Jesus is personal, but that is not to say that it's a private matter. Paul reminds the Philippians that one day all worldly powers and authorities will speak the name of Jesus and will confess that "Jesus Christ is Lord" (Phil 2:9–11). To confess Jesus as Lord means to acknowledge him as the one who shares the identity of Israel's God. In the Old Testament Scriptures God is named YHWH, *Kyrios*, Lord; and in the New Testament Jesus is revealed as the one who bears that name. So to confess Jesus as Lord is to set him above all other loyalties. It is to make a universal claim. If Jesus truly shares the identity of YHWH, then he is the hidden truth of creation, of history, and of every human life (Col 1:15–17). I confess him as *my* Lord only because I recognize him as *the* Lord.

Such a universal claim might sound insensitive or even oppressive to modern pluralistic ears. And it is true that Christians have at times used the universality of the gospel to justify oppression and injustice. Rightly understood, however, the message of Jesus' lordship is a word of comfort and hope for all people.

In the ancient church, the confession of Jesus' lordship began to change the way Christians thought about slavery. Christianity took root in societies that were rigidly stratified and hierarchical. There were clearly marked distinctions between men and women, rich and poor, Jews and gentiles, slaves and free. But the Christian community did not accept that people were defined by those social distinctions. All came to the same baptismal waters and confessed the same Lord. When they entered naked into the waters of baptism, no one could tell the difference between rich and poor, slave and free.

So even when the Christian movement had barely begun, we find Paul urging a believer to regard his Christian slave as "no longer a slave ... but a beloved brother" (Phlm 16). By the fourth century, Gregory of Nyssa issued a scathing denunciation of the institution of slavery. Gregory didn't have access to modern ideas of individual rights and liberties. As he saw it, the problem with slavery was that it creates a false lordship. By making one person the master of another, human beings claim an authority that belongs only to God. As Gregory says to the slave owner, "you have forgotten the limits of your authority." The world has only one Lord—and this Lord "does not enslave," but "calls us to freedom."[17]

Because Jesus is the universal Lord, all worldly power is limited and provisional. Because he is Lord, social distinctions are relativized and will ultimately be set aside completely. All people owe their allegiance not to any other person but to Jesus. Before him they are able to recognize one another as sisters and brothers. And so the logic of universal lordship gives rise to an egalitarian ethic.

The ancient institution of slavery didn't vanish all at once. But when slaves and free persons stood side by side and confessed that Jesus is Lord, the days of slavery were numbered. When early believers entered the waters and took the name of Jesus on their lips, the tectonic plates shifted. The slow revolution had begun.

"WHO WAS CONCEIVED BY THE HOLY SPIRIT"

At the beginning of Luke's Gospel, the angel visits Mary and tells her that "the Holy Spirit will come upon you, and the power of the Most High will overshadow you" (Luke 1:35). This opening act of Jesus' story is meant to remind us of another beginning: "In the beginning God created the heavens and the earth. Now the earth was formless and empty, darkness was over the surface of the deep, and the Spirit of God was hovering over the waters" (Gen 1:1–2 NIV).

Creation occurs when the Spirit of God broods over the formless abyss and brings forth life out of nothing. Elsewhere the Old Testament writers speak of the divine Breath or Spirit as the source of creation: "When you send forth your spirit, they are created" (Ps 104:30). When God forms Adam from the ground in the second creation story, the man is at first a lifeless clay sculpture. But then God breathes spirit into the clay, and it becomes a living being (Gen 2:7).

So when the Spirit broods over the womb of Mary, we see a picture of God's creative work happening all over again. Jesus is brought into being by the creative breath of God's Spirit. A Christian pastor in the second century, Hippolytus, said that in the Virgin's womb the Son of God "refashioned the first-formed Adam in himself."[18] The first Adam led the human race astray. But here is a new Adam, a new beginning for the human family, a new ancestor who will lead us into life and joy.

In the third century, Origen of Alexandria came up with a striking image to illustrate the way Jesus' humanity was united to the eternal Son of God. He pictured a piece of iron placed in a fire until it is glowing with heat. This iron, he says,

has become wholly fire, since nothing else is discerned in it except fire; and if anyone were to attempt to touch or handle it, he would feel the power not of iron but of fire. In this way, then, that soul [that is, Jesus' human soul] which, like iron in the fire, was placed in the Word forever, in Wisdom forever, in God forever, is God in all that it does, feels, and understands.[19]

Jesus is truly human: nothing but iron. He is truly divine: nothing but fire. Jesus is so permeated by the divine presence that every part of his humanity is filled with divine energy.

He is born of a woman: he is conceived by God's Spirit. He is human: he is divine. He is iron: he is fire.

This way of thinking about Jesus' humanity and divinity is really just an attempt to make sense of the complex things that are said about Jesus in the Gospels. The Gospels portray Jesus as someone whose life is drawn directly from the source of God's own creative energy. Even in his mother's womb, he is already the bearer of the Holy Spirit. In Luke's Gospel, the same Spirit that brooded over Mary's womb is always flashing out and touching the lives of those who come into contact with Jesus. When Mary greets her cousin Elizabeth, the baby in Elizabeth's womb leaps for joy and Elizabeth is filled with the Holy Spirit (Luke 1:41). In the sixth century, the Syrian preacher Jacob of Serug described the scene like this:

> The Son of God sent forth the Spirit ... and the boy was baptized by the Holy Spirit while he was still in his mother's womb. At once the confined babe began preaching to prepare the way for the King who came from the house of David. A new message was heard from within the womb, a babe who leaps and exults and hurries to prepare the way.[20]

It is the same Spirit who flashes out when the woman with the flow of blood touches the hem of Jesus' clothes and is instantly healed (Matt 9:20–22). It is the same Spirit who, when Jesus lies dead in the tomb, breathes life into his body so that death is dissolved and the grave is emptied (Rom 8:11).

And it is the same Spirit that flashes out on the day of Pentecost so that tongues of fire descend on Jesus' friends and they are transformed from a lifeless rabble of frightened followers into fearless witnesses of the resurrection (Acts 2:1–4). The same Spirit who rested on Jesus in his mother's womb now rests on the whole company of Jesus' followers.

Jesus is the bearer of the Spirit and the sender of the Spirit. In him, the Spirit creates a new beginning for the whole human race. That is what the church proclaims in the concise but astonishing words of the ancient catechism: "conceived by the Holy Spirit."

"BORN OF THE VIRGIN MARY"

"I can't believe that!" said Alice.

"Can't you?" the Queen said in a pitying tone. "Try again: draw a long breath, and shut your eyes."

Alice laughed. "There's no use trying," she said: "one *can't* believe impossible things."

"I daresay you haven't had much practice," said the Queen. "When I was your age, I always did it for half-an-hour a day. Why, sometimes I've believed as many as six impossible things before breakfast."[21]

here are Christians today who take a similar view of the virgin birth. To them, the idea of the virgin birth is a relic of bygone days when people were simpler and found it easier to believe in impossible things.

We can handle the rest of the creed, but the virgin birth stretches credulity too far.

The trouble starts when we take this line of the creed and view it in isolation. It would be like finding a bicycle chain if you had never seen a bicycle. You would struggle to make sense of the strange object: what is it for? Is it a weapon? Or an uncomfortable piece of jewelry? To understand the bicycle chain you have to see it in its proper context. It's the same with the virgin birth. If we take it in isolation we might conclude that it's just a spectacular miracle or even a logical absurdity. And then it becomes a sheer effort to try to believe it—as if saying the baptismal creed were the same as trying to believe six impossible things before breakfast.

To understand the virgin birth we need to see how it fits into the whole story of Scripture—a story in which miraculous births play a starring role.

Israel's story begins with a promise to Abraham and Sarah (Gen 12–17). A couple who cannot conceive are chosen by God and told that they will have a great family. Sarah laughs at the promise. But later, when she has given birth in her grand old age, the child is named Laughter (Hebrew: Isaac) because of the astonished joy of his parents. Sarah can hardly believe her own body: and yet it's true. She has given birth to the promise.

The next great turning point in Israel's story is the arrival of Moses (Exod 2:1–10). Although Moses' conception is not a miracle, his infancy is marked by a miraculous escape from danger. He is snatched away from the murdering hand of Pharaoh. He is placed in a basket and set adrift on the river, where he is found and adopted by a member of the royal household, an Egyptian princess who then appoints the baby's biological mother to be his nursing maid. The whole story portrays an amazing providential design by which Moses is spared and, as it were, smuggled right into the heart of Egyptian power. All this is meant to anticipate the great miracle to come when God will deliver the people of Israel from slavery.

When Israel has come to the promised land, before the establishment of the monarchy, God raises up judges to lead the people. The greatest of the judges is Samson, and his story begins with another miraculous birth (Judg 13:1–25). Samson's mother is unable to conceive. But she is visited by an angel who tells her that she will give birth to a savior who will triumph over the Philistines.

After the age of the judges comes the age of the prophets and kings. It begins with Hannah, a woman full of grief because she cannot bear children (1 Sam 1:1–20). In answer to her prayer, Hannah becomes miraculously pregnant and her child Samuel becomes the prophet who will anoint the first kings of Israel. With the miraculous birth of Samuel the whole line of Hebrew prophets comes into being.

That is how it goes in the Old Testament: at the great turning points of history, we find a woman, pregnant, and an infant child brought into the world by the powerful promise of God. Israel's story is a story of miraculous births.

Later the people of Israel were taken from the promised land and led away into Babylonian captivity. It was the darkest hour of their history. Out of the depths of despair, the promise of God was heard again through the prophet Isaiah. The prophet compared the coming deliverance to the joy of a miraculous pregnancy:

> Sing, O barren one who did not bear;
> burst into song and shout,
> you who have not been in labor!
> For the children of the desolate woman will be more
> than the children of her that is married, says the LORD.
> Enlarge the site of your tent,
> and let the curtains of your habitations be stretched out;
> do not hold back; lengthen your cords
> and strengthen your stakes.
> For you will spread out to the right and to the left,
> and your descendants will possess the nations
> and will settle the desolate towns. …
> All your children shall be taught by the LORD,
> and great shall be the prosperity of your children.
>
> (Isa 54:1–3, 13)

It is as if Israel, in her exile, has been a poor woman in a small tent with room for only one. But now it's time to make alterations on her home, to prepare the space for a bustling family. The one who has never been in labor is about to give birth. That is what the promise of God looks like.

It is not hard to see why pregnancy and childbirth played such an important role in the history of God's covenant with Israel. God's overarching plan is to bring blessing to all the nations through the descendants of Abraham. If ever the Hebrew women ceased to bear children, the promise would have failed: the whole world would be lost. Pregnancy and childbirth are the means by which God's promise makes its way through the crooked course of history. Every newborn child is a reminder of the promise. Every male child was physically marked by circumcision: a potent reminder that their bodies were not merely their own but had been scripted into a bigger story.

Against this backdrop it should come as no surprise to find Israel's Messiah entering the world by means of a miraculous pregnancy. In the Gospel of Luke, the first character we meet is another faithful Jewish woman who can't conceive: Elizabeth. Like Samson's mother, Elizabeth was promised that she will bear a child (Luke 1:5–25).

After Elizabeth has become pregnant, we meet her cousin Mary. An angel tells Mary that she too will miraculously conceive and that her child will be the fulfillment of all God's promises to Israel. Mary responds with simple trust and gladness. The joy of her Magnificat (Luke 1:46–55) is the same joy that made Sarah laugh when she gave birth to Isaac. It is the same joy that wiped away Hannah's tears when she gave birth to Samuel. Israel's joy—the joy of God's promise, the joy of salvation—is all summed up in that startling experience of the birth of a miraculous child.

The confession that Jesus Christ was born of a virgin isn't just a bit of theological eccentricity. It's not a random miracle story. It's a reminder that our faith has deep roots in Israel's story and Israel's Scriptures. The coming of the Savior wasn't just a new thing. It was the culmination of the whole great story of God's loving faithfulness to the people of Israel. When we confess that Jesus is "born of the Virgin Mary," we see him silhouetted against the backdrop of God's promise to Abraham, the exodus from Egypt, the rule of the judges, the coming of the prophets, and the promised deliverance from exile.

The meaning of history is not power and empire, but promise and trust. The secret of history is revealed when a woman, insignificant to the eyes of the world, responds in joy to God's promise and bears that promise into the world in her own body.

"SUFFERED"

ntil now, you would think the creed was describing a perfect world. It has spoken of the God who creates the world and then enters into that world through the womb of a woman. So far there is no hint that anything is wrong. The Apostles' Creed makes no mention of the fall or original sin. But now we hear ourselves confessing the word "suffered," and with a painful jolt we realize all is not well.

When God comes into the world in the person of Jesus, God is met with violent resistance. The creatures have turned against their Creator. The loving Creator of the world has been cast out. The judge of the earth has come among us: we have judged him and put him on the gallows. "He came unto his own, and his own received him not" (John 1:11 KJV). There is room in our world, it seems, for everything—except God.

Among Christian scholars today, one of the main criticisms of the Apostles' Creed is that it contains no account of the life and ministry of Jesus. The reading of the Gospel stories has always been central to the life of the Christian community. The creed was never intended as a substitute for the four Gospels but only as a guide to the faithful reading of them. Whenever we read Jesus' story we are to keep in mind that he was born of a woman, that he was a flesh-and-blood human being. And when we read his story we are to keep in mind that he wasn't just another human being, but was "God's only Son, our Lord," the living self-expression of God's will. That is what the creed offers: some general guidelines for the faithful reading of the Gospels. The creed doesn't try to include all the details but only to remind us of the larger narrative and to focus our attention on Jesus' identity as divine and human, the Son of God and Mary's son.

Still, it's not quite true that the creed just ignores everything that happens between Jesus' birth and death. In fact, already among the earliest Christians it had become customary to sum up Jesus' whole life under one word: "suffering." We can already see that in the Gospels themselves: "Was it not necessary that the Messiah should suffer these things?" (Luke 24:26). Luke records that Paul summed up Jesus' life in the same way: "It was necessary for the Messiah to suffer" (Acts 17:3). By the time of the later New Testament writings, the word "suffering" has become a convenient formula for referring to the whole story of Jesus' life and death: "he suffered" (Heb 2:18).

This abridgement of Jesus' story is no substitute for the unbroken rhythm of reading and rereading the testimony of the four Gospels. But it is a tried-and-true safeguard against certain kinds of misreading. When ancient people heard the gospel they were tempted to think of Jesus as a supernatural spirit, untouched by physical life. For them, it was especially important to be reminded that Jesus is a human Lord who "suffered in the flesh" (1 Pet 4:1).

Christians today might be more tempted by the allure of a triumphalist faith, or by a distorted gospel that promises worldly satisfactions and success. But we are baptized into the way of a suffering Lord who lays on his followers not a crown but a cross. We will share Christ's glory, yes—to the extent that we also share in his sufferings (Rom 8:17).

"UNDER PONTIUS PILATE"

I t is so easy to forget what the Christian faith is really about. We might slip into the assumption that it is a kind of philosophy, a comprehensive view of life and the world. Debates with atheists are often carried out on this level. We give the impression that Christianity has to be cleverer than atheism if it is to be true. Or we might assume that the Christian faith is essentially a religious doctrine, a set of accurate beliefs about God. Scholars and students are especially vulnerable to this assumption. We start out trying to get a clearer understanding of our beliefs, and before long we have come to feel that those beliefs, if they are to be true, have to be flawlessly integrated into a theological system.

There is some truth in all this. But such approaches become misleading whenever they give the impression that Christianity is essentially a theory. If Christianity is a theory, then salvation is ultimately an intellectual matter. It is about getting rid of the wrong ideas and acquiring the right ones.

The Apostles' Creed is concerned with doctrine. The ancient catechism was meant to help believers get a clear outline of the teaching of Scripture. There are some underlying doctrinal patterns in the creed: belief in God as Father, Son, and Holy Spirit; and belief in creation's goodness, its redemption, and its final glorification. Still, it's important to notice that the creed isn't a list of concepts and ideas. At the center of the creed is a story, or at least the summary of a story. We are meant to take our bearings not just from doctrine but from history: from a sequence of events that occurred in a particular time and place.

That's how one of history's most dubious characters, Pontius Pilate, finds his way into the creed. He enters the creed "like a dog into a nice room," as the twentieth-century theologian Karl Barth put it.[22] The name of Pontius Pilate is a historical anchor. It prevents us from turning the Christian faith into a set of general truths about the world. It reminds us that the gospel is not an idea but a fact.

The baptismal confession centers on a name: the name of Jesus. And in case we start to think that "Jesus Christ" is a theoretical concept, the creed adds a second name: "Jesus—the one who suffered under Pontius Pilate." Pontius Pilate is there to remind us that God has acted at a particular moment in human history. The salvation of the world can be dated. Certain people were there when it happened.

The heart of Christianity is not an idea but a brute fact. Not a theory but a particular human life. Not a general principle but a person with a name: Jesus, who suffered under Pontius Pilate.

Because Jesus himself is at the center, the continuous reading of the four Gospels is the central spiritual discipline of the Christian life. The story of Jesus is read whenever believers assemble. In the sacraments of baptism and the Lord's Supper we participate communally in Jesus' story, remembering and repeating the events of his life through a liturgical reenactment. In prayer we repeat verbatim the words that Jesus taught his followers to say: "Our Father ..." (Matt 6:9–13). When we serve the marginalized, the poor, and the oppressed, we are not just following a general principle of compassion but are giving a fresh dramatic performance of the script of Jesus' life. In a sermon on the love of the poor, the fourth-century preacher Gregory of Nazianzus appealed to his congregation:

> While we may, let us visit Christ, let us heal Christ, let us feed Christ, let us clothe Christ, let us welcome Christ, let us honor Christ. ... Since the Lord of all will have mercy and not sacrifice ... , let us offer to him through the poor who are today downtrodden.[23]

It is as if each new believer becomes another character in the gospel story. Each one has a part to play. Jesus still lives, and his story still continues in the lives of his followers. The church calendar, too, is just an elaborate way of remembering and repeating Jesus' story year after year. We read the Gospels not only with our minds but also with our lives.

Really there are as many unique performances of the story of Jesus as there are believers. But each one remains accountable to the history narrated in the four Gospels. We all respond differently to Jesus' story, but the story itself does not change. The same Jesus, born of Mary and condemned by Pilate, is always at the center. All the church's practices and institutions are ultimately attempts to respond to that person. All the mysteries of faith are rooted in the events of history. That is why one of history's villains, Pontius Pilate, lives in the memory of the church and will be confessed until the end of the world whenever a person is baptized into the way of Jesus.

"WAS CRUCIFIED"

In the Roman Empire, crucifixion wasn't only about death. It was about public disgrace. The problem with getting yourself crucified wasn't just that it would kill you but that it would humiliate you at the same time. Modern readers of the New Testament might assume that the worst thing about crucifixion was the physical suffering. But in a culture of honor and shame, the pain of the soul—humiliation—can be even worse than the pain of the body.

The psalms of Israel often lament over the experience of humiliation. Psalm 79 describes the sack of Jerusalem by a neighboring army:

> O God, the nations have come into your inheritance;
> they have defiled your holy temple;
> they have laid Jerusalem in ruins.

They have given the bodies of your servants
to the birds of the air for food,
the flesh of your faithful to the wild animals of the earth.
They have poured out their blood like water
all around Jerusalem,
and there was no one to bury them.

(Ps 79:1–3)

This list of horrors culminates in the worst fate of all: public disgrace.

We have become a taunt to our neighbors,
mocked and derided by those around us.

(Ps 79:4)

It is as if to say: we have been butchered—and, what's worse, humiliated! Jesus went to his death reciting a psalm of humiliation:

My God, my God, why have you forsaken me? ...
I am a worm, and not human;
scorned by others, and despised by the people.
All who see me mock at me;
they make mouths at me, they shake their heads.

(Ps 22:1, 6–7)

To be crucified was to be cast out of the human community, rejected by God and the world. It was literally a fate worse than death.

The humiliation of Jesus' death made a deep impression on his early followers. Quoting an early Christian hymn, Paul describes the whole life of Jesus as a descent into humiliation and disgrace. "He emptied himself, taking the form of a slave"; he "humbled himself and became obedient to the point of death—even death on a cross" (Phil 2:7–8). Jesus descended to the lowest rung on the social ladder. He became a slave and died a slave's death. Though he possessed the highest honor, he embraced the worst disgrace. The world was saved by Jesus' shame: that is the scandalous message of the cross.

Jesus' followers were the first people in the history of the world to describe humility as a virtue. Paul reminds the Philippian believers that they ought to have the "same mind" as Christ (Phil 2.5), renouncing honor and becoming like slaves in service to one another. In ancient Roman culture, the whole purpose of life was to acquire honor and to shun whatever might diminish one's reputation. To be humble was the worst thing that could happen to a person. Yet the earliest Christians scorned pride and elevated humility. Paul calls himself a "slave of Jesus Christ" (Rom 1:1), as if such slavery were the highest honor in the world.

The message of a humble Lord was a shocking thing to hear in the ancient world. Yet today if anyone is asked whether it's better to devote one's life to self-aggrandizement or to service, most would admit that a life of service is better. The message of the cross has inverted the ancient values of honor and shame.

Jesus' shocking claim that it is better to serve than to be served (Mark 10:45) is accepted today as if it were plain common sense. We take it for granted that nurses and carers deserve special respect, and that the poor and powerless have a special dignity.

Because, today, the virtue of humility is taken for granted, we no longer feel the original scandal of the gospel. We are no longer offended by Jesus' shame. But it was his shameful death that passed judgment on the world's moral order and laid bare a new order of righteousness. Up has become down; down has become up. In Jesus, God

> has brought down the powerful from their thrones,
> and lifted up the lowly;
> he has filled the hungry with good things,
> and sent the rich away empty.

(Luke 1:52–53)

"DIED, AND WAS BURIED"

hristians confess that the death of Jesus is the turning point of history. The New Testament authors have many different ways of describing the meaning of that death. Through his shameful death, Jesus attains the highest honor (Phil 2:6–11). By succumbing to mortality he makes human nature immortal (1 Cor 15:42–57). His death is the world's life (Rom 5:12–21). It is the darkness that illuminates, the judgment that does not condemn (John). It is a defeat that ushers in God's sovereign reign (Mark). It is a termination that inaugurates a new epoch in history (Luke–Acts). It is a fulfillment that totally surpasses what was promised (Matthew). It is a sacrifice that dissolves the entire sacrificial system from within (Hebrews). It is a violent catastrophe that triumphs over the violence of human history (Revelation).

These are not exactly straightforward explanations. They are paradoxical expressions, each pointing back to the brute fact of Jesus' death without exhausting the meaning of that event.

Paul's theme of union with Christ was especially important in later Christian teaching about Jesus' death. According to Paul, Jesus has shared all that is ours so that we may share all that is his. He shares our poverty and we share his riches (2 Cor 8:9). He stands under the curse that is rightly ours, and we stand under the blessing that is rightly his (Gal 3:6–14). By uniting himself with us, he is identified completely with our sin and we are identified with his righteousness (2 Cor 5:21). The idea here is not so much substitution as mutual participation: God and humanity are perfectly united in the person of Jesus so that each partakes of all that belongs to the other.

About a hundred years after Paul, the second-century theologian Irenaeus developed the same logic by arguing that we could not have been redeemed unless every aspect of our human condition was embraced by the Son of God:

> He did not reject human nature or exalt himself above it. … Becoming an infant among infants, he sanctified infants; becoming a child among children, he sanctified those having this age … ; becoming a young adult among young adults, he was an example for young adults and sanctified them to the Lord. … Lastly, he came even to death so that he might be "the Firstborn from the dead,"

himself "holding primacy in all things" (Col 1:18), the Author of life, prior to all and going before all.[24]

The Son of God heals our nature by joining it to himself. Human nature is changed by this union. Mortality joins hands with immortality. The grave becomes the beginning of life.

The mysterious connection between birth and death was explored by Gregory of Nyssa in a fourth-century address to new believers preparing for baptism. Gregory pointed out that Jesus would not really have shared our nature if he had not also shared its limits. Everyone comes into the world through the womb and departs into the tomb. And so the Son of God embraced our humanity at these extreme limits. In Gregory's words:

> The birth makes the death necessary. He who had decided to share our humanity had to experience all that belongs to our nature. Now human life is encompassed within two limits, and if he had passed through one and not the other, he would only have half fulfilled his purpose. … Our whole nature had to be brought back from death. Thus he stooped down to our dead body and stretched out a hand, as it were, to one who lay prostrate. He approached so near death as to come into contact with it.[25]

Because, in Jesus, God has fully shared our condition, there is no human experience that can alienate us from God. Every affliction is an opportunity to identify with Jesus, to "suffer with him so that we may also be glorified with him" (Rom 8:17). Even dying becomes another way of following Jesus and of identifying with him. We die differently because the Son of God has touched our frail mortality and has drawn it into the wider context of his life. We die differently because we know that "neither death, nor life ... will be able to separate us from the love of God in Christ Jesus our Lord" (Rom 8:38–39).

Each one of us approaches the day of our death. But there is someone waiting for us there: Jesus, the Lord of life, who meets us at all life's crossroads, at the beginnings and ends of all our ways.

"HE DESCENDED INTO HELL; ON THE THIRD DAY HE ROSE AGAIN FROM THE DEAD"

"I f I make my bed in Sheol, you are there" (Ps 139:8). The message of the Bible is that death is not the end. Death does not defeat God's promise. Death is not separation from God. In Jesus, God has dwelt among the dead. God has touched the very limits of our nature, from birth to death, in order to sanctify us and to unite us to God. The Living has embraced the dead. Death has been subsumed by life.

Several of the New Testament authors describe Jesus' death as a descent into the world of the dead. "When he ascended on high he made captivity itself a captive," after having first "descended into the lower parts of the earth" (Eph 4:8–9). He "went and made a proclamation to the spirits in prison," and then went "into heaven and is at the right hand of God" (1 Pet 3:18–22). Christ's word is proclaimed among the dead. His name is confessed "under the earth," among the dead (Phil 2:9–11). The dead are not lost forever. They are not condemned to silence. In Jesus, "the dead will hear the voice of the Son of God, and those who hear will live" (John 5:25). Because of him, the emptiness of death has been filled with God's fullness.

Eastern Orthodox iconography is especially attentive to this aspect of Christian hope. In Orthodoxy, the icon of the resurrection portrays a glorified Christ standing over the broken doors of hell. Beneath his feet, the chains and locks that have held the dead are all broken. The doors of hell have come unhinged. The grave has been emptied. An old man and an old woman are depicted on either side of Christ. They are Adam and Eve. Christ has seized them by the wrists and raised them up from the shadowy underworld.

Jesus descends into hell because that is where we have fallen. The fourteenth-century English writer Julian of Norwich put it like this:

> For Jesus is all who shall be saved and all who shall be saved are Jesus. … For he went into hell, and when he was there he raised up out of the deep deepness the great root of those who were truly knit to him in high heaven.[26]

The Son of God has taken our nature to himself. He allows our fallen nature to drag him down. He descends to the very abyss of the human condition. He traces our plight right back to the

root and takes hold of us there. He embraces our humanity at the point of its total collapse into nonbeing.

Because he shares our nature he is able to fall with us into death; because he is the Son of God he is able to fill death with his presence so that the grave becomes a source of life. In Christ, the dead are united to God and are alive in the strength of that union. The resurrection is not just an isolated miracle that happens to Jesus. It is something that happens to us—to Adam and Eve, to me, to the human family. As Jesus rises, the whole of humanity rises with him.

In the ancient church, the message of Christ's triumph over death produced some peculiar attitudes toward the dead. Believers would assemble for prayer in tombs. They would worship Christ among the bones of the dead. Believers would raise the bodies of martyrs in the air and parade them through the streets like trophies. At funerals they would gaze lovingly on the dead and sing psalms of praise over their bodies. Such behavior shocked their pagan neighbors. According to Roman law, the dead had to be buried miles away from the city so that the living would not be contaminated. But Christians placed the dead right at the center of their public gatherings. The earliest church buildings were really just big mausoleums erected over the remains of the martyrs. The tombs of the saints were, in the words of John Chrysostom, "tombs with life, tombs that give voice."[27]

When new believers were preparing for baptism, they would gather in the presence of the dead, and there they would receive instruction in the ancient catechism. Even today the Apostles' Creed makes the most sense when you imagine the words echoing among the bones of the catacombs. The creed is marked everywhere by an unflinching acceptance of the facts of human mortality, coupled with a straightforward confidence in the ultimate triumph of life—a triumph that has already happened once and for all in the person of Jesus.

Where others see only defeat, Jesus' followers see a paradoxical victory. Where others see only contamination, we see the sanctification of human nature. Where others see only darkness and despair, we see broken gates. Where others see an end, we see new beginnings. Death is serious: but not as serious as life. It has been placed in a wider context of meaning. We bury our dead under the sign of the cross. We lay our bones to rest not in horror but in peace. The dominant sound at a Christian funeral is not mourning but the singing of praise.

Death is no longer the ultimate power in this world. In the ancient church, the martyrs were seen as a special proof of that. In the fourth century, Athanasius compared the martyrs to children who play with a lion in the desert:

> If you see children playing with a lion, don't you know that the lion must be either dead or completely powerless? In the same way … when you see Christ's believers playing with death and despising it, there can be no doubt that death has been destroyed by Christ and

that its corruption has been dissolved and brought to an end.[28]

In the death and resurrection of Jesus, death itself was altered. And now, says Athanasius, "we no longer die as those condemned but as those who will arise."[29]

By nature we are all on the way from birth to death. But by grace we are traveling in the opposite direction. The Christian life is a mystery that moves from death to birth. At the beginning we are baptized into Christ's death; and at the end we are born into the life of the resurrection. We are born as though dying; we die as those who are being born.

Where, O death, is your victory?
Where, O death, is your sting?

(1 Cor 15:55)

"HE ASCENDED INTO HEAVEN AND IS SEATED AT THE RIGHT HAND OF THE FATHER"

he dualistic sects of the second century had a distaste for some parts of the Gospel tradition, including the stories of Christ's ascension (Mark 16:19; Luke 24:51; Acts 1:9–11). Marcion's edited version of the Gospel of Luke had omitted both the birth narrative and the ascension. This was because Marcion imagined a spiritual, disembodied savior, and he forced the Scriptures to conform to that vision. Other teachers claimed that Christ ascended spiritually, leaving his physical body behind. In such doctrines, the body is believed to be evil; the material world is consigned to ruin; salvation is about escaping the misery of this world. Jesus himself (so it was said) wanted nothing to do with physical life in this world; he came to bring enlightenment and to liberate the human spirit from its bondage to the world of creation.

It was against such teaching that the early Christians proclaimed a gospel of Christ's bodily incarnation, bodily suffering, bodily death, bodily resurrection, and bodily ascension. The faith of the ancient church was not about spiritual escape but about the redemption and transfiguration of human life in its fullness, including the life of the body. As Irenaeus said it in the second century, the Son of God "did not reject human nature or exalt himself above it," but united himself with our nature in order to unite us to God.[30]

When the New Testament writers speak of the ascension, they are not describing Jesus' absence but his sovereign presence throughout creation. He has not gone away but has become even more fully present. His ascent "to the right hand of the Father" is his public enthronement over all worldly power. No scriptural passage is quoted so often in the New Testament as Psalm 110:1:

> The LORD says to my Lord,
> "Sit at my right hand
> until I make your enemies your footstool."

The earliest Christians proclaimed that Jesus had been enthroned as the universal Lord and messiah. The exalted Christ has "entered his glory" (Luke 24:26; 1 Tim 3:16). From now on, "all things are subject" to his authority (Phil 3:21; Heb 2:8). Because he is ascended, his life is universally available. His loving authority extends over the whole creation and is present wherever believers assemble (Eph 1:20–23). He "has gone into heaven and is at the right hand of God, with angels, authorities, and powers made subject to him" (1 Pet 3:22).

So the ascension is not meant to make us wonder where Jesus has gone. Instead it ought to elicit the psalmist's question,

> Where can I go from your spirit?
> Or where can I flee from your presence?
>
> (Ps 139:7)

In a painting by the Australian Aboriginal artist Shirley Purdie, the ascension of Jesus is shown not as a flight into the sky but as a triumphant ascent into the red earth. He "ascends down," so to speak, into the land—not fleeing our world but entering into its depths in order to exercise his loving authority over (and within) the whole creation.[31] That is a profound depiction of the New Testament understanding of the ascension. Because Jesus has ascended, he is even nearer to us and to all things. "In him all things hold together, ... and through him God was pleased to reconcile to himself all things" (Col 1:17–20).

And through our union with Christ, we share also in his ascension. The lives of believers are now forever located "in Christ," as Paul so often says. When Jesus ascends to the Father, he takes our humanity with him. To quote Irenaeus again, because Jesus has ascended we also "ascend through the Spirit to the Son, and through the Son to the Father."[32] In Jesus, our nature has taken up residence in the presence of God.

"AND HE WILL COME TO JUDGE THE LIVING AND THE DEAD"

o judge is to discriminate, to separate one thing from another. The Gospel of John portrays Jesus as the light of the world. The same light shines on everyone, but there are different ways of responding to it. Some walk gladly into the light while others screw their eyes shut and remain in darkness. "And this is the judgment, that the light has come into the world, and people loved darkness rather than light" (John 3:19). That is what it means for Jesus to bring judgment. It is not that he is gracious to some and angry toward others. Jesus is "full of grace and truth" (John 1:14), but grace itself divides those who encounter it.

When the ancient Christians talked about divine judgment, they were careful to avoid the impression that there are two different gods, a god of wrath and a god of grace. That line of thinking would lead straight to the theological nightmares of Gnosticism. For Christians, there is no division within God. "God is light and in him there is no darkness at all" (1 John 1:5). The one face of God is revealed in Jesus.

Some early Christian teachers suggested that heaven and hell might in fact be the same place. Isaac the Syrian, a monk and preacher of the seventh century, argued that all people are ultimately brought into the presence of divine love. But "the power of love works in two ways": it is a joy to some but a torment to others.[33] Teachers sometimes witness a similar phenomenon in the classroom. The same class can be a delight for one student and a torment for another. One is excited; the other is bored. Both students are in the same place, and both are listening to the same teacher. But one is in heaven and the other is in hell. That is how Isaac the Syrian imagines the world to come: not as two different places but as two different ways of responding to the love of God. "Those who are punished in hell," Isaac writes, "are scourged by the scourge of love. For what is so bitter and vehement as the punishment of love?"[34]

The judgment that Christ brings, moreover, is not just a division between two kinds of people. When Christ's light shines into our lives, it creates a division within ourselves. None of us is entirely good or entirely bad. Each of us is a mixture. The bad grows up in our lives like weeds among the wheat, and the two are so closely entwined that in this life we can't easily tell the difference (Matt 13:24–30). Sometimes our worst mistakes turn out to produce good fruit. And sometimes we discover that our virtues have produced unforeseen collateral damage. Our lives are not transparent to ourselves. We cannot easily tell where the bad ends and the good begins.

So it is a comfort to know that one day someone else will come and lovingly separate the good from the bad in our lives. The confession that Christ will come as judge is not an expression of terror and doom. It is part of the good news of the gospel. It is a joy to know that there is someone who understands all the complexities and ambiguities of our lives. It is a joy to know that this one—the only one who is truly competent to judge—is "full of grace and truth" (John 1:14). He comes to save, not to destroy, and he saves us by his judgment.

The fourth-century writer Gregory of Nyssa composed an imagined dialogue with his older sister Macrina—"my teacher," as he liked to call her. The dialogue discusses the body, the soul, and the resurrection. It depicts divine judgment as a painful but necessary purification in which each person is finally set free to respond fully to the love of God:

> The divine judgment ... does not primarily bring punishment on sinners. ... It operates only by separating good from evil and pulling the soul toward communion in blessedness. It is the tearing apart of what has grown together which brings pain to the one who is being pulled.[35]

Jesus will come to judge the living and the dead. That will be the best thing that ever happens to us. On that day the weeds in each of us will be separated from the wheat. It will hurt—no doubt it will hurt—when our self-deceptions are burned away. But the pain of truth heals; it does not destroy. On our judgment day we will be able for the first time to see the truth of our lives, when we see ourselves as loved.

I BELIEVE IN THE HOLY SPIRIT,

the holy catholic church,
the communion of saints,
the forgiveness of sins,
the resurrection of the body,
and the life everlasting.

Amen,

"I BELIEVE IN THE HOLY SPIRIT"

T he story of the Bible begins with the Spirit brooding over the abyss, ready to bring forth creation out of nothing (Gen 1:2). And at the turning point of the ages we find the Spirit brooding over the womb of a virgin (Luke 1:35). The Spirit rests on Mary's body in order to bring forth the new Adam, the beginning of a new creation.

The language of the creed reminds us that the work of this creative Spirit is not yet finished. The same Spirit is now brooding over the whole human race, bringing forth a new human community in the image of Christ.

One of the great themes of the Bible is the unity of the human family. In the garden of Eden, God makes a man and a woman, a miniature society imprinted with God's own image. And the Bible ends with depictions of a future city where people from every tribe and tongue will live together in a perfect harmony of praise (Rev 7:9).

In Genesis, the fall brings about a tragic disordering of human relationships. There is a curse now at the heart of the relation between man and woman, as well as between parents and children. The relation between humans and the rest of creation is likewise blighted (Gen 3:14–19). God's creation is divided. Each human being is a fragment torn loose from the whole.

This grim assessment of human fallenness culminates in the story of Babel (Gen 11:1–9). Here, human beings have begun to use their collective life to mock God. And so God divides their language, making it impossible for them to work together. They can no longer share a common world or articulate a common good. They cannot form a coherent society. Each group is a mere splinter of humanity, all scattered across the cursed earth, exiled and alone.

But with the coming of Jesus, the story of Babel is reversed. When the Spirit descends on the frightened company of Jesus' followers, they all begin to speak in different languages. The multicultural crowd outside is astonished to find that each one's language is being spoken by a band of Galileans. They ask, "How is it that we hear, each of us, in our own native language?" (Acts 2:1–13).

The Pentecost story shows the undoing of the fall through the creation of the Christian community. There is now a new human society in which all the old divisions are torn down. That is what happens when the Spirit is present. The Spirit fulfills the Creator's original plan by bringing forth a universal community whose boundaries are as wide as the world. The Spirit broods over the chaos of human nature, lovingly piecing the fragments back together so that together we form an image of the Creator.

Paul notes that the presence of the Spirit is marked by heightened individuality as well as a deeper communal belonging. The Spirit fuses unity and diversity by bringing "many gifts" together in "one body" (1 Cor 12:12–31). We become more truly ourselves as the Spirit broods over us and as our lives are knit together with other lives and stories.

In this way the Spirit broods over each of Christ's followers, renewing the human race one life at a time and drawing all into a common family. Basil, a great fourth-century Cappadocian pastor and social reformer, explained it like this: the Spirit "is like a sunbeam whose grace is present to the one who enjoys it as if it were present to that one alone, yet it illuminates land and sea and is mixed with the air."[36] There is nothing more personal, and more universal, than the Holy Spirit.

"THE HOLY CATHOLIC CHURCH"

At baptism each believer proclaims that the church is "catholic." The word simply means universal. It means that there is only one church because there is only one Lord. Though there have been many Christian communities spread out across different times, places, and cultures, they are all mysteriously united in one Spirit. Each local gathering of believers is a full expression of that mysterious catholicity.

The church is catholic because it is a microcosm of a universal human society. In the waters of baptism, all the old social divisions are made irrelevant. The church includes every kind of person: rich and poor, male and female, Jew and gentile, slave and free (Gal 3:26–28). Whatever defined a person before is relativized by the new defining mark of membership in the company of Jesus' followers. The thirteenth-century Italian theologian Thomas Aquinas explained that the message of Jesus is universal "because no one is rejected, neither lord nor servant, neither male nor female."[37] There is no social barrier that could exclude a person from inclusion in this body. The boundaries of the church are as wide as the human race.

Further, the church is catholic because it preaches a catholic message. The gospel is not addressed to one particular social class or ethnic group. It is addressed to every imaginable human being. There is nobody in the world for whom the message of Jesus could be irrelevant. One of the most unusual aspects of the Christian faith is its translatability. The other great monotheistic traditions, Judaism and Islam, place a high value on preserving the divine message in its original language, whether Hebrew or Arabic. But right from the start, the Christian movement was marked by translation. Jesus himself spoke Aramaic, but the four Gospels all translated his teaching into vernacular Greek so that the message would be available to as many readers as possible. Within a remarkably short time the Christian movement had taken root in many different cultures, each one reading and proclaiming the gospel message in its own tongue. The message of Jesus is a catholic message.

The message of the gospel is also "catholic" in the way it responds to the human plight. The deepest human needs are addressed in the gospel. The message of Jesus doesn't just speak to a special part of life—the moral or spiritual part, for example. It speaks to the whole person, body and soul, individual and social. It is a catholic message because it embraces the whole person in a word of grace and truth. The gospel is as broad and deep as human life itself. It is a catholic word because it speaks to the whole human condition.

But there is an even more radical dimension of Christian catholicity. The greatest barrier that divides human beings from one another is not culture or language or class. The greatest barrier is death. It splits the human family into the two classes of the living and the dead. All other social divisions are petty compared to this great division. All human beings are powerless before this fundamental boundary. But in the resurrection Jesus has stepped across the barrier and restored communion between the living and the dead. He has formed one family that stretches out not only across space but also across time. The body of Christ is the most inclusive community imaginable because it includes not only those who are now living but also all believers who have ever lived.

The message of the gospel is directed not primarily to individuals but to this new community. God's plan of salvation all along has been to create one human society as the bearer of the divine image. In that sense, the church isn't just the way people respond to salvation; the church *is* salvation. The church is what God has been doing in the world from the beginning. It is a representative microcosm of what God intends for the whole human family.

That is why every division between believers is a denial of the gospel. A Christian community is catholic to the extent that it is always uniting. Wherever we identify a line of division within the human family, the risen Jesus calls us to step across that line in the power of the Spirit. For "there is one body and one Spirit, just as you were called to the one hope of your calling, one Lord, one faith, one baptism, one God and Father of all" (Eph 4:4–6).

"THE COMMUNION OF SAINTS"

Sometime in the second century, a Greek philosopher named Celsus wrote a book attacking the Christian faith. Nearly a hundred years later, the great Egyptian scholar Origen was asked to reply to Celsus's criticisms. Origen dutifully composed a big book that is perhaps still the finest work of Christian apologetics ever written. But before launching into his defense of the faith, Origen pointed out that the way of Jesus doesn't really need any defense. He wrote:

> Jesus is always being falsely accused, and there is never a time when he is not being accused. … He is still silent in the face of this and does not answer with his own voice. But he makes his defense in the lives of his genuine disciples, for their lives cry out the real facts and defeat all false charges.[38]

Jesus wrote no books. He established no institutions. He did not lay down the right answers to moral questions. He did not seem particularly interested in founding a new religion. He was the author not of ideas but of a way of life. Everything Jesus believed to be important was entrusted to his small circle of followers. What he handed on to them was simply life. He showed them his own unique way of being alive—his way of living, loving, feasting, forgiving, teaching, and dying—and he invited them to live the same way.

Becoming a Christian is not really about institutional membership or about adopting a system of ideas. To become a Christian is to be included in the circle of Jesus' followers. I am washed with the same bath that Jesus and all his followers have had. I get to share the same meal that Jesus shared with his followers. Four of Jesus' followers left written records of what he said and what he was like, and I get to spend my life continually pondering those four accounts. I read them not because I am studying ideas about Jesus but because I am studying *him*. I want everything in my life, right down to the smallest and most disappointing details, to enter somehow into communion with the life of Jesus.

I share the holy bath and the holy meal, and I read the holy stories, because I am seeking Jesus. But when I do these things I am also seeking myself. I want to find myself among the circle of Jesus' followers. I want to be wherever Jesus is—and he is in the company of his friends. I want my whole life to be "hidden with Christ in God" (Col 3:3). I want my life's small story to be tucked into the folds of Jesus' story.

When this happens, my life acquires a meaning beyond itself. I begin to see myself as part of a great company, an ever-widening circle of people who have handed their lives over to the pattern of Jesus' life. This great company of disciples seems to speak with one voice, to breathe with one Spirit, to cry "Abba, Father!" with one unceasing prayer (Rom 8:15–16).

The Fourth Gospel ends by telling us that it has offered only a glimpse of Jesus. If everything Jesus did was written down, "the world itself could not contain the books that would be written" (John 21:25).

Perhaps, at the end of the age, the Total Gospel will be read out and will be found to contain everything—every life, every story, every human grief and joy, all included as episodes in the one great, infinitely rich story of Jesus and his friends. The world itself is too small for such a book. Life and death are too small for the communion of saints.

"THE FORGIVENESS OF SINS"

he confession of the forgiveness of sins was a relatively late addition to the creed. The earliest baptismal confessions spoke simply of "the Holy Spirit, the holy church, and the resurrection of the flesh."

But a dramatic debate arose among fourth-century believers about the nature of sin and forgiveness. Christians in those days were still subjected to periods of persecution under the Roman emperors. In 303 the emperor Diocletian ordered that the property of Christians was to be seized, their books burned, and their places of worship destroyed. All Christian leaders were to be imprisoned. Only those who sacrificed to the Roman gods would be released. Some Christians were martyred. But martyrdom was always the exception. Countless frightened Christians—including, of course, many clergy—came out to make the sacrifices. The emperor even permitted the Christians to sacrifice en masse, making it as easy as possible for them to renounce their faith.

By offering public sacrifice to the Roman gods, such Christians had effectively renounced their baptism. But before long things returned to normal, and Christianity was again tolerated as part of Rome's pluralistic empire. Predictably, the apostate believers, known as "traitors," soon came back to church as if nothing much had happened.

This situation created a pastoral crisis for many congregations. What is to be done with believers who have renounced their baptism? Can they be accepted back into the faith? Is there a public way of marking their reentry into the church? Should they be baptized a second time? Or should they be permanently excluded from participation in the Christian community?

Even more awkward was the question about clergy who had made the pagan sacrifices. When ministers of Christ invalidate their faith, does it mean that their ministry has been invalid all along? What if you had been baptized by a minister who later renounced his faith? Would you need to get baptized again by someone else?

These were difficult questions. It was a time of intense soul-searching for many believers. Through this struggle over the "traitors," the deepest questions of Christian identity came sharply into focus. What is it that makes you a follower of Christ? And what can you do if you have strayed from Christ's path? Is the Christian community a church of the pure (as some called it), or can struggling, weak, uncertain souls also find a place within that community?

The fourth-century crisis led eventually to clear answers to these questions. Christian teachers argued that the church includes everyone who confesses Jesus and receives baptism. It is not only for the pure and the spiritually successful. Failures in discipleship—even dramatic public failures—do not exclude a person from the grace of God. As Augustine insisted in one of his many sermons against spiritual elitism: "We must never despair of anyone at all."[39] When backslidden believers return to the faith, they don't need to be rebaptized. They simply need to show, through a changed way of life, that they are trying to take their baptism seriously. There is no need to be baptized more than once, since that would imply that we need to be forgiven more than once. The forgiveness of sins has taken place once for all in the death and resurrection of Jesus.

These conclusions were so important that the ancient church began to include "the forgiveness of sins" as part of the baptismal confession. In 381 the Nicene Creed was expanded to include the statement "we acknowledge one baptism for the forgiveness of sins."

A church that takes its stand on the forgiveness of sins can never be a church of the pure. It will always be a community that is patient and understanding toward the timid and the imperfect. Whenever a judgmental, elitist spirit enters into the Christian community, we need to hear again the confession: "I believe in the forgiveness of sins."

We believe that we stand not by our own achievements but by the achievement of Jesus' death and resurrection. We believe that the spiritually strong and the spiritually weak are both sustained by the same forgiving grace. We believe that we rely solely on grace, not only in our worst failures but also in our best successes. We believe that if ever we should turn away from grace, if ever our hearts grow cold and we forget our Lord and become unfaithful to his way, he will not forget us. His faithfulness is deeper than our faithlessness. His yes is stronger than our no. In a seventh-century sermon on God's mercy, Isaac the Syrian said:

> As a handful of sand thrown into the great sea, so are the sins of all flesh in comparison with the mind of God. And just as a strongly flowing stream is not obstructed by a handful of dust, so the mercy of the creator is not stemmed by the [sins] of his creatures.[40]

"THE RESURRECTION OF THE BODY"

rom start to finish, the creed affirms the value of the material world. In opposition to rival systems of thought that denigrate matter and the body, the ancient catechism confesses God as the maker, redeemer, and sanctifier of this world. The life of the flesh is not alien to God. It is God's creature and the object of God's loving intentions.

The first part of the creed proclaims God as the creator of all things, not only of the spiritual world but of the material world too: "maker of heaven and earth."

The second part of the creed confesses that the Son of God has become part of this world by taking human nature to himself. Ancient gnostic teachers viewed the bodies of women with the utmost horror; but for Christians, the womb of a woman is the sacred venue of the divine action in this world. All God's intentions for creation come into focus here: "conceived by the Holy Spirit, born of the Virgin Mary." And the Son of God suffers in the flesh. He is crucified. He dies. He is buried. He is raised in the flesh and continues to share our nature in the glory of the resurrection.

The third part of the creed confesses that God's Spirit remains present in the midst of this world. Believers share in the power and presence of the Holy Spirit. The Spirit does not live on some higher plane but is here with us. The Spirit "befriends the body"[41] so that the life of the resurrection begins to appear already in our ordinary lives. And the life that we anticipate now, in the Spirit, is the life that we also await with eager hope.

Belief in bodily resurrection is one of the controlling undercurrents of the New Testament. Yet the nature of the resurrection is hardly ever addressed directly. The Gospel accounts never try to depict the resurrection itself. Mark's account does not even include a depiction of the risen Jesus: the tomb is empty, and it is left to the reader to understand why (Mark 16:1–8).[42] The other Gospels depict the risen Jesus, but not the event of resurrection itself (Matt 28; Luke 24; John 20). The tomb is already empty when the disciples get there. The resurrection has occurred in secret. It has happened—where? In the tomb? In hell? In eternity? Wherever and however it happened, the event has already occurred. That is why the disciples are faced with a decision, whether to believe or not.

The closest the New Testament comes to explaining the resurrection is Paul's discussion in 1 Corinthians 15. His argument is that we too will rise in the same way that Christ is risen. But we don't have any clear picture of what a resurrection looks like. So Paul tries to explain it using the image of a seed (1 Cor 15:35–49). The body now is like a seed, and the life of the resurrection is like the tree. There is an unimaginable difference between the seed and the tree. They do not look alike. You would not be able to guess the appearance of the tree by looking at the seed. Yet their identity is the same. In the same way, Paul says, our mortal bodies will be planted and will be raised immortal in Christ. Paul calls this "a mystery" (15:51). In the coming life we will be the same identical persons that we are now—yet unimaginably different. "We will all be changed, in a moment, in the twinkling of an eye" (15:51–52).

In this passage Paul explains the meaning of the resurrection by not-explaining it. He points to the mystery of the seed and the tree and offers that mystery as an explanation. He leads our minds right to the edge of what can be grasped or imagined.

So what are we really claiming to believe when we say that we believe in the resurrection of the body? In a third-century sermon,[43] Origen noted that the baptismal confession does not speak of "the resurrection of bodies" but "the resurrection of the body"—singular. Perhaps, he suggests, what is raised up on the last day will not be individuals but the body of Christ, a single person that incorporates the whole of humanity with Jesus at its head. Origen's line of reasoning is based partly on Ezekiel's vision of the valley of dry bones. What the prophet sees in this vision is not a multitude of individual resurrections but one corporate resurrection of "the whole house of

Israel" (Ezek 37:11). In the same way, Christian hope is never just hope for myself. It is a social hope. It is hope for humanity. The only future that I may legitimately hope for is a future that also includes my neighbor.

As his sermon continues, Origen goes a step further. He says that if Jesus is the head, then he must be waiting for his body to assemble. It is as if Jesus' resurrection were still incomplete. "His joy waits," Origen says, until the whole body of humanity has been raised. If all the world were redeemed except one person, there would still be something missing in the joy of Jesus. He would continue to wait. The festivities would be on hold. He would not yet drink the cup of the kingdom.

If God's intention is to bring forth a single redeemed body, then the eternal joy of the life to come depends, in some measure, on each of us. The joy of Jesus is on hold until we take up our place with him. That is the remarkable conclusion that Origen reaches in his sermon.

This still leaves us no closer to being able to form a clear picture of the life of the world to come. So what do Christians hope for? Perhaps it is enough to say that Christian hope is a social and therefore an embodied hope, and that this hope centers on communion with the person of Jesus. We learn these things not by speculating about the afterlife but by contemplating the risen Jesus and accepting by faith the things that are revealed in him. Most of all, what we know about Jesus is that he is the *philanthropos*, the lover of humanity. And so the life that we await will be a life of love.

"AND THE LIFE EVERLASTING"

There is nothing especially appealing about the thought of living forever. The Argentine writer Jorge Luis Borges tells the story of a man who drinks from a river of immortality and becomes immortal. But without death, life lacks definition; it doesn't mean anything. One day the man learns of another river that can take immortality away. And so for centuries he wanders the earth and drinks from every spring and river, seeking to end the curse of endless life. "Death," writes Borges, "makes men precious and pathetic; their ghostliness is touching; any act they perform may be their last."[44]

You cannot make life better just by increasing its quantity. What matters most is quality. It's perhaps regrettable that our English version of the creed speaks of "the life everlasting"—as if life just goes on and on for an indefinitely long time. A better translation would be "eternal life." The creed uses an expression that is found frequently in the New Testament, especially in the Gospel of John. For John, "eternal life" is about quality, not quantity. It is a quality of life that believers experience already when they attach themselves to Jesus. "Whoever believes in the Son has eternal life" (John 3:36). "Anyone who hears my word and believes him who sent me has eternal life" (John 5:24).

John does not really define this special quality of life, except by saying that it is identical with Jesus himself. The Son of God is the one who is truly and fully alive. All other living things are alive through him (John 1:3–4). "Eternal life" can even be used as a title for Jesus. He is called "the eternal life that was with the Father" (1 John 1:2). When we get close enough to this personal life source, we begin to share his quality of life. We too become truly and fully alive. "And this is eternal life, that they may know you, the only true God, and Jesus Christ whom you have sent" (John 17:3).

So when we confess that we believe in eternal life, we're not talking about the duration of life but about a relationship. In the person of Jesus, we find ourselves drawn into a quality of life that is so rich that it can only be described as eternal. Jesus says, "I came that they may have life, and have it abundantly" (John 10:10).

When lovers embrace, they feel sometimes that time has stopped and that the whole world is smaller than the space of their small room. An intense experience of love can alter our ordinary perceptions and seem to lift us beyond the limits of space and time. That is why so many poets and philosophers speak of the "eternal" quality of love. And it is why every experience of love has something tragic about it too: we feel that we have transcended time, yet we know it cannot last. Love is fragile and fleeting. Time reaps everything away in the end.

Perhaps eternal life is something like that intense experience of love, but without the shadow of tragedy. When we experience life in its fullness, death is rendered obsolete. Jesus says, "I am the resurrection and the life. Those who believe in me, even though they die, will live, and everyone who lives and believes in me will never die" (John 11:25–26). Jesus is so truly and fully alive that, to him, even death is really another way of being alive. When we find our way to the living source of life, to Jesus himself, we discover that death is not really death anymore. Even in death our relationship to Jesus is not broken. Death becomes another place where we can go to find him. Wherever we go, he waits to meet us there.

In the thirteenth century, Francis of Assisi composed his famous hymn, "The Canticle of the Sun."[45] Francis sees everything in the light of God's love, and so he sees every creature as a friend. He sings praise to Brother Sun and Sister Moon, Brother Fire and Sister Water. And after spreading his joy over the whole creation, he turns to "Sister Death" and greets even her as a friend. Francis has forgotten how to be afraid. He has found his way to the source of life. He meets Jesus everywhere, even in death, and so he never really dies but only enters more deeply into life.

The lovers embracing in their room forget that time is passing or that the outside world exists. Fleetingly, they rise above time to an eternal moment. What would it mean for the whole of life to be caught up in such a moment? Perhaps we would not even notice that death had been overcome. We would be too preoccupied by life and love. Irenaeus describes eternal life as a kind of blessed forgetfulness. One day, he says, believers will share so fully in the life of God that "they will forget to die."[46]

"AMEN"

I have been trying in these pages to explain the faith of the Apostles' Creed. But I have only scratched the surface. Every line of the creed reaches down into the mystery of the gospel. We are dealing here with words of faith—words whose meaning cannot be fully comprehended, even though a coherent vision of the world rises into view as we say them. No mind has yet grasped the creed in all its fullness, just as "no one has yet breathed all the air."[47]

So it is strange that we end the creed by pronouncing a solemn "amen." To say amen to the creed is to sign my name to it. I confirm the truth of this: I authorize it: amen. Yet we barely fathom what we are saying in the creed. How could anyone have the power to say amen to all this?

A friend told me once that he always crosses his fingers when he gets to the line about the virgin birth. I replied, "What? You mean the rest of the creed is so easy that you can say it with uncrossed fingers? Does the rest of it make perfect sense to you? Do you mean to say that you can verify the truth of everything else—creation, incarnation, resurrection, the last judgment—all except the virgin birth?"

Is there anyone who never feels a flicker of doubt when they contemplate the mysteries of faith? Can anyone really say the amen with all their heart? Isn't it really here, at the last word of the creed, that we ought to cross our fingers? Shouldn't we end the creed by saying: "Oh boy, I hope so!" How can anyone have the audacity to say "Amen"?

When Paul wrote to the church at Corinth, he said:

> As surely as God is faithful, our word to you has not been "Yes and No." For the Son of God, Jesus Christ, whom we proclaimed among you ... was not "Yes and No"; but in him it is always "Yes." For in him every one of God's promises is a "Yes." For this reason it is through him that we say the "Amen," to the glory of God.
>
> (2 Cor 1:18–20)

The whole creed is about God's action, God's agency, God's initiative. Even at the end, when we pronounce the amen, we are drawing not on our own resource but God's. We are participating in the action of Jesus, who looks into the face of God and sees all God's ways and works, and says: "Yes! Amen!" When we say the creed, we echo his mighty and eternal amen with our own small, hopeful voices.

And so we're back where we started: with the mystery of the "I" that speaks in the creed. Who is this "I"? Whose voice is it that says "I believe" and then pronounces the authoritative "amen"?

The trend in many churches today has been to replace the "I" with the communal "we." The assumption is that it's individualistic to say "I" and that switching to the plural helps to foster a sense of community and corporate identity. Thus the creed is amended—corrected?—to say, "We believe." In the same way, hymns are sometimes updated to reflect the preference for the communal "we."

Interestingly, the early Christians had exactly the opposite view. In an exposition of Psalm 121, Augustine argued that the "I" is the proper symbol of corporate worship, while the use of "we" is individualistic:

> Let [the psalmist] sing from the heart of each one of you like a single person. Indeed, let each of you be this one person. Each one prays the psalm individually, but because you are all one in Christ, it is the voice of a single person that is heard in the psalm. That is why you do not say, "To you, Lord, have we lifted up our eyes," but "To you, Lord, I have lifted up my eyes." Certainly you must think of this as a prayer offered by each of you on his or her own account, but even more you should think of it as the prayer of the one person present throughout the whole world.[48]

Augustine's point is that the church is not a collection of atomistic individuals. It's not just a matter of many different voices joining together to sing a psalm or say the creed. Rather, the church speaks with one voice. It is intensely personal when I say "I believe." I say the creed as if the words applied to me alone. But beneath and within and around my own personal "I," I hear the surge of a greater voice. There is a corporate "I" in which my own voice participates. This corporate "I" is the body of Christ—which really means Christ himself as the unifying head of a new human society. In Augustine's view it is ultimately Christ who prays and sings and declares the amen. "All the members of Christ, the body of Christ diffused throughout the world, are like a single person asking God's help, one single beggar, one poor suppliant. And this is because Christ himself is that poor man, since he who was rich became poor."[49]

In the same way, the faith that we proclaim at baptism is ultimately the faith of Jesus himself. He is the one who truly turns to God and trusts in God fully. In baptism we are immersed into his faith. We are included in his unique relationship to God. When we say "I believe" we are speaking in him, just as it is really his voice speaking in us by the Holy Spirit when we cry out "Abba, Father." We participate in Jesus' own response to God when we confess and pray and join our voices to his amen.

In the Gospels, Jesus often begins his sayings with the striking preface: "Amen, amen, I tell you …"[50] He alone has the authority to pronounce the amen. He says the amen not in agreement to anyone else's word but as an expression of his own authority. His word is truth, not because it meets any external criteria of truthfulness but because he is himself the standard against which all other claims to truth are measured. It is he who looks into the depths of God and tells us what he sees. His word is Yes and Amen. In fact, the book of Revelation goes so far as to name him "the Amen, the faithful and true witness" (Rev 3:14). In him the amen to God has become personified.

And so at the end of the creed we join our voices to his—what else could we do?—and allow ourselves to be caught up in Jesus' own response to God. "I believe ... Amen!" And all to the glory of God—Father, Son, and Holy Spirit.

ENDNOTES

1. Irenaeus, *Against the Heresies* 1.10.1.
2. Hippolytus, *On the Apostolic Tradition*, 133–36.
3. Irenaeus, *Against the Heresies* 1.10.1.
4. Irenaeus, *On the Apostolic Preaching* 1.1.7.
5. Using the distinction of J. L. Austin in *How to Do Things with Words*.
6. Augustine, *Confessions* 6.5.7.
7. Augustine, *Sermon* 118.1.
8. Athanasius, *Against the Pagans* 29.
9. Gregory of Nazianzus, *Oration* 31.7.
10. Gregory of Nazianzus, *Oration* 29.16.
11. Athanasius, *On the Council of Nicaea* 24.
12. Tertullian, *Against Praxeas* 10.
13. Augustine, *Exposition of Psalm* 58.1.10.
14. Sarah Coakley, *Powers and Submissions*, 37.
15. See Adolf von Harnack, *Marcion: The Gospel of the Alien God.*
16. Gregory of Nyssa, *Catechetical Oration* 7; in *Christology of the Later Fathers.*
17. Gregory of Nyssa, *Fourth Homily on Ecclesiastes* 335.11.
18. Hippolytus, *Commentary on Daniel* 4.11.
19. Origen, *On First Principles* 2.6.6.

20. Jacob of Serug, *On the Mother of God* 50–51.
21. Lewis Carroll, *Through the Looking Glass*, chapter 5.
22. Karl Barth, *Dogmatics in Outline*, 108.
23. Gregory of Nazianzus, *Oration* 14.40.
24. Irenaeus, *Against the Heresies* 2.22.4.
25. Gregory of Nyssa, *Catechetical Oration* 32.
26. Julian of Norwich, *Revelations of Divine Love*, chapter 51.
27. John Chrysostom, *Homily on Saint Eustathius* 4; in *The Cult of the Saints*.
28. Athanasius, *On the Incarnation* 29.
29. Athanasius, *On the Incarnation* 10.
30. Irenaeus, *Against the Heresies* 2.22.4.
31. The painting, titled "Ngambuny Ascends," is discussed in Rod Pattenden, "Seeing Otherwise: Touching Sacred Things," 24–25.
32. Irenaeus, *Against the Heresies* 5.36.2.
33. Isaac the Syrian, *Homily 28*.
34. Isaac the Syrian, *Homily 28*.
35. Gregory of Nyssa, *On the Soul and the Resurrection* 84.
36. Basil, *On the Holy Spirit* 9.22.
37. Thomas Aquinas, *Sermon-Conferences of St. Thomas Aquinas on the Apostles' Creed*, 129.
38. Origen, *Contra Celsum*, 4.
39. Augustine, *Exposition of Psalm* 36.2.11.
40. Isaac the Syrian, *Homily 51*.
41. Eugene F. Rogers, *After the Spirit*, 70.
42. Assuming that the shorter ending of Mark's Gospel is authentic.
43. Origen, *Homily 7 on Leviticus*.
44. Jorge Luis Borges, "The Immortal," in *Collected Fictions*, 192.
45. The most popular English version is William Henry Draper's paraphrase, "All Creatures of Our God and King."
46. Irenaeus, *Against the Heresies* 5.36.2.
47. Gregory of Nazianzus, *Oration* 30.17.
48. Augustine, *Exposition of Psalm* 122.2.
49. Augustine, *Exposition of Psalm* 39.28.
50. Often translated "truly, truly" or "very truly" in English Bibles.

CHURCH FATHERS
TRANSLATIONS USED

Athanasius. *Contra Gentes and De Incarnatione*. Translated by Robert W. Thomson. Oxford: Clarendon, 1971.

———. *On the Incarnation*. Translated by John Behr. Popular Patristics. Crestwood, NY: St. Vladimir's Seminary Press, 2011.

———. *On the Council of Nicaea (De Decretis)*. In *Athanasius*. Translated by Khaled Anatolios. London: Routledge, 2004.

Augustine. *Confessions*. Translated by Maria Boulding. The Works of St. Augustine: A Translation for the 21st Century I/1. 2nd ed. Hyde Park, NY: New City Press, 2012.

———. *Expositions of the Psalms*. Translated by Maria Boulding. The Works of St. Augustine: A Translation for the 21st Century III/15–20. 6 vols. Hyde Park, NY: New City Press, 2000–2004.

———. *Sermons 94A–147A*. Translated by Edmund Hill. The Works of St. Augustine: A Translation for the 21st Century III/4. New York: New City Press, 1992.

Basil. *On the Holy Spirit*. Translated by Stephen Hildebrand. Popular Patristics. Crestwood, NY: St. Vladimir's Seminary Press, 2011.

Chrysostom, John. *The Cult of the Saints*. Translated by Wendy Mayer. Popular Patristics. Crestwood, NY: St. Vladimir's Seminary Press, 2006.

Gregory of Nazianzus. *On God and Christ: The Five Theological Orations*. Translated by Frederick Williams and Lionel Wickham. Popular Patristics. Crestwood, NY: St. Vladimir's Seminary Press, 2002.

———. *Select Orations*. Translated by Martha Vinson. Fathers of the Church. Washington, DC: Catholic University of America Press, 2003.

Gregory of Nyssa. *On the Soul and the Resurrection*. Translated by Catharine P. Roth. Popular Patristics. Crestwood, NY: St. Vladimir's Seminary Press, 1993.

———. *An Address on Religious Instruction*. In *Christology of the Later Fathers*, edited by Edward Rochie Hardy, 268–325. Library of Christian Classics. London: SCM, 1954.

———. *Homilies on Ecclesiastes*. Edited by Stuart George Hall. Berlin: Walter de Gruyter, 1993.

Hippolytus. *Kommentar zu Daniel*. Edited by Marcel Richard. Vol. 1.1 in *Hippolyt Werke*. Berlin: Academie Verlag, 2000.

———. *On the Apostolic Tradition*. Edited by Alistair C. Stewart. Popular Patristics. 2nd ed. Crestwood, NY: St. Vladimir's Seminary Press, 2015.

Irenaeus. *Against the Heresies*. Translated by Dominic J. Unger. New York: Newman Press, 1992–2012.

———. *On the Apostolic Preaching*. Translated by John Behr. Popular Patristics. Crestwood, NY: St. Vladimir's Seminary Press, 1997.

Isaac the Syrian. *The Ascetical Homilies of Saint Isaac the Syrian*. 2nd ed. Boston: Holy Transfiguration Monastery, 2011.

Jacob of Serug. *On the Mother of God*. Translated by Mary Hansbury. Popular Patristics. Crestwood, NY: St. Vladimir's Seminary Press, 1998.

Origen. *On First Principles*. Translated by John Behr. 2 vols. Oxford: Oxford University Press, 2017.

———. *Contra Celsum*. Translated by Henry Chadwick. Cambridge: Cambridge University Press, 1953.

———. *Homilies on Leviticus, 1–16*. Translated by Gary Wayne Barkley. Fathers of the Church. Washington, DC: Catholic University of America Press, 1990.

Tertullian. *Against Praxeas*. Translated by Ernest Evans. London: SPCK, 1948.

WORKS CITED

Austin, J. L. *How to Do Things with Words*. Cambridge, MA: Harvard
    University Press, 1962.

Barth, Karl. *Dogmatics in Outline*. Translated by G. T. Thomson. London:
    SCM, 1949.

Borges, Jorge Luis. "The Immortal." In *Collected Fictions*, translated by
    Andrew Hurley, 183–95. New York: Penguin, 1998.

Carroll, Lewis. *Through the Looking Glass*. London: Penguin, 1994.

Coakley, Sarah. *Powers and Submissions*. Oxford: Blackwell, 2002.

Harnack, Adolf von. *Marcion: The Gospel of the Alien God*. Translated by
    John E. Steely and Lyle D. Bierma. Durham: Labyrinth, 1990.

Julian of Norwich. *Revelations of Divine Love*. Translated by Elizabeth
    Spearing. London: Penguin, 1998.

Pattenden, Rod. "Seeing Otherwise: Touching Sacred Things." In
    Indigenous Australia and the Unfinished Business of Theology, edited
    by Jione Havea, 17–30. New York: Palgrave Macmillan, 2014.

Rogers, Eugene F. *After the Spirit*. Grand Rapids: Eerdmans, 2005.

Thomas Aquinas. *Sermon-Conferences of St. Thomas Aquinas on the Apostles'
    Creed*. Translated by Nicholas Ayo. Notre Dame: University of
    Notre Dame Press, 1998.

SCRIPTURE INDEX

Old Testament

New Testament

NAME INDEX

The Christian Essentials series is set in TEN OLDSTYLE, designed by Robert Slimbach in 2017. This typeface is inspired by Italian humanist and Japanese calligraphy, blending energetic formality with fanciful elegance.

CHRISTIAN ESSENTIALS

The Christian Essentials series passes down tradition that matters. The ancient church was founded on basic biblical teachings and practices like the Ten Commandments, baptism, the Apostles' Creed, the Lord's Supper, the Lord's Prayer, and corporate worship. These basics of the Christian life have sustained and nurtured every generation of the faithful—from the apostles to today. The books in the Christian Essentials series open up the meaning of the foundations of our faith.